T0199044

STEVEN M.F. COHEN

I WILL ALWAYS BE WITH YOU

Illustrated by
OLHA MAKSYMTSIV

To order additional copies of this book, contact:
Xlibris
844-714-8691
www.Xlibris.com
Orders@Xlibris.com

ISBN: Softcover   978-1-6641-4916-8
          Hardcover   978-1-6641-4917-5
          EBook   978-1-6641-4915-1

Print information available on the last page

Rev. date: 12/21/2020

Dedication Page

This book is dedicated to my grandson
For Tucker
God Will Always Be With You.
Peace & Joy my baby boy.
Grandpapa loves you so very much!

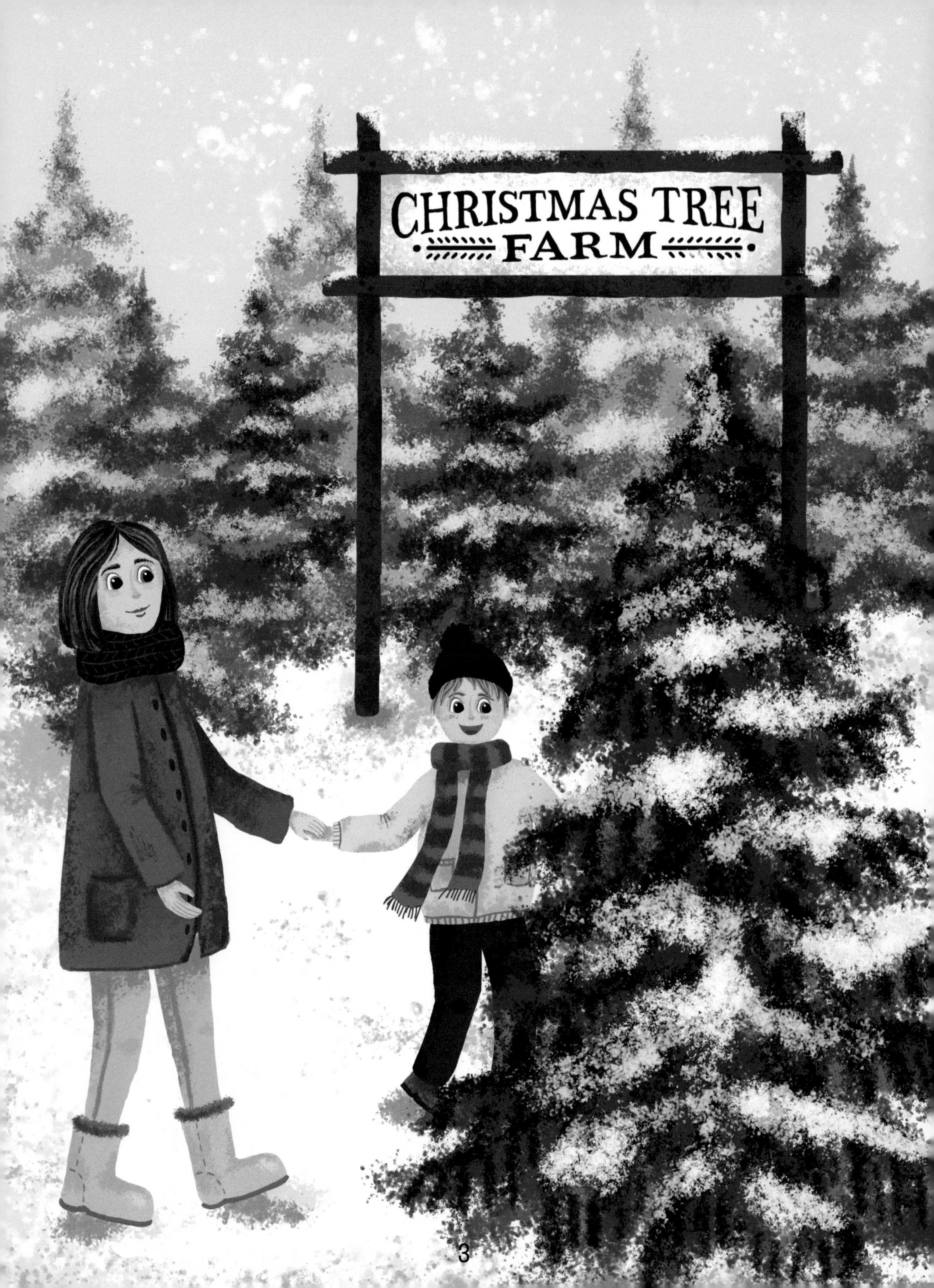
CHRISTMAS TREE
FARM

For Santa

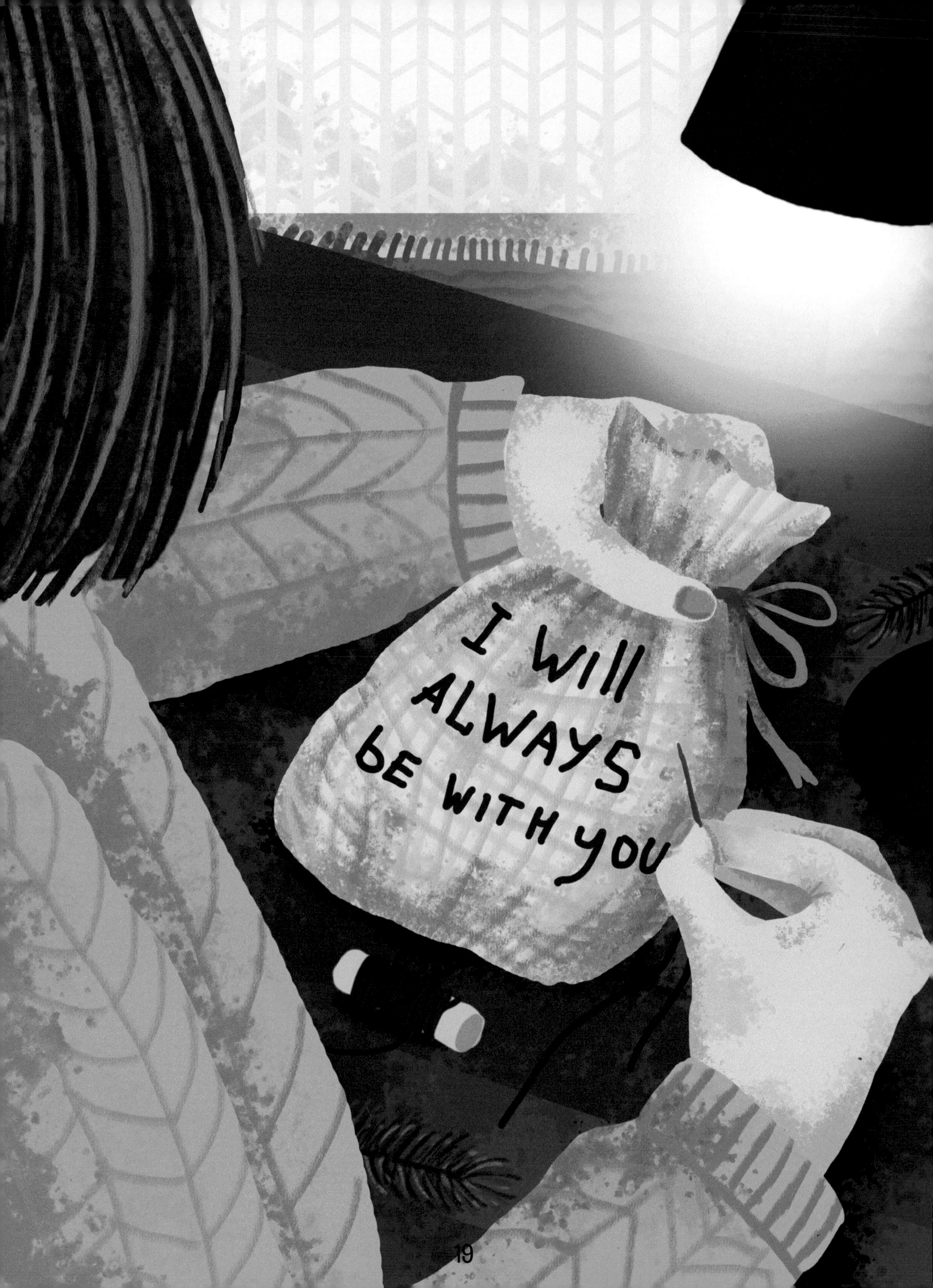
I will
ALWAYS
be WITH YOU

20

Printed in the United States
By Bookmasters